A Mark Dahle Portfolio

Monkey Brains In Big Desert

Little Gibbon's Big Adventures #4

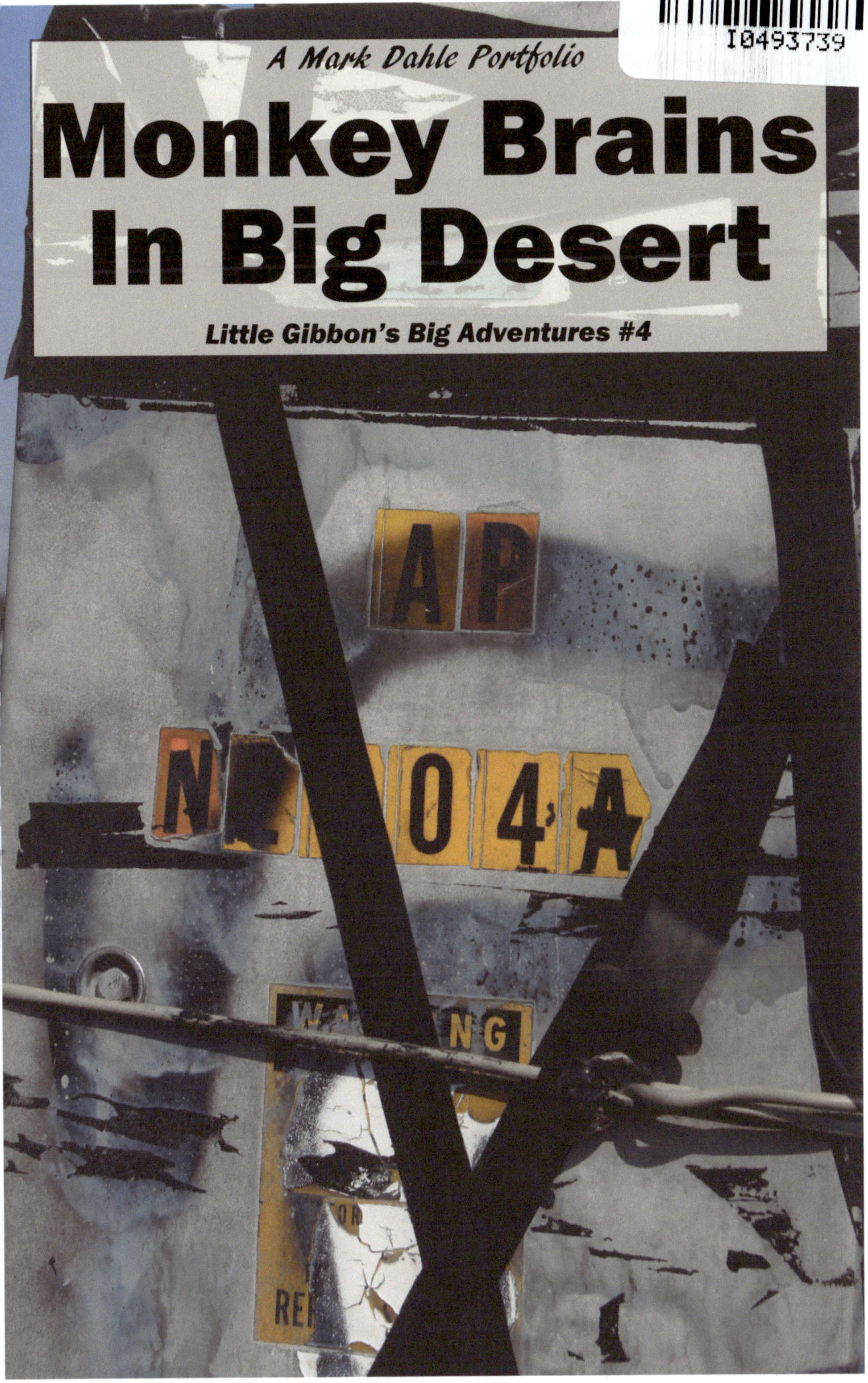

This is the fourth story about a gibbon who liked adventures. All the other gibbons called him Monkey Brains.

Books in this series include:
1. Monkey Brains On Big River
2. Monkey Brains On Big Ocean
3. Monkey Brains On Big Mountain
4. Monkey Brains In Big Desert

~ ~ ~

Mark Dahle Portfolios can be read in a few minutes and enjoyed for a lifetime.

Unlike many picture books, the text in this book is not related to the art. This might seem weird at first. One thing that makes it better is to order more portfolios until you get used to it. Fortunately, space is provided on the pages for you to draw your own pictures of Big Desert if you like.

This portfolio includes a beautiful 36 x 24 inch painting (at the right), twenty-five great photos of Eastern Washington, and a story about an adventurer who called himself Little Gibbon. Photographs in this book are available in limited editions. See http://www.MarkDahle.com for more information and for previews of upcoming portfolios.

We do our best to create portfolios free of editing mistakes. But it's hard to catch everything. We reward people who report errors in any Mark Dahle portfolio. For details see MarkDahle.com/Typos.html or email MarkDahle@aol.com with the subject line "Typos." Thanks!

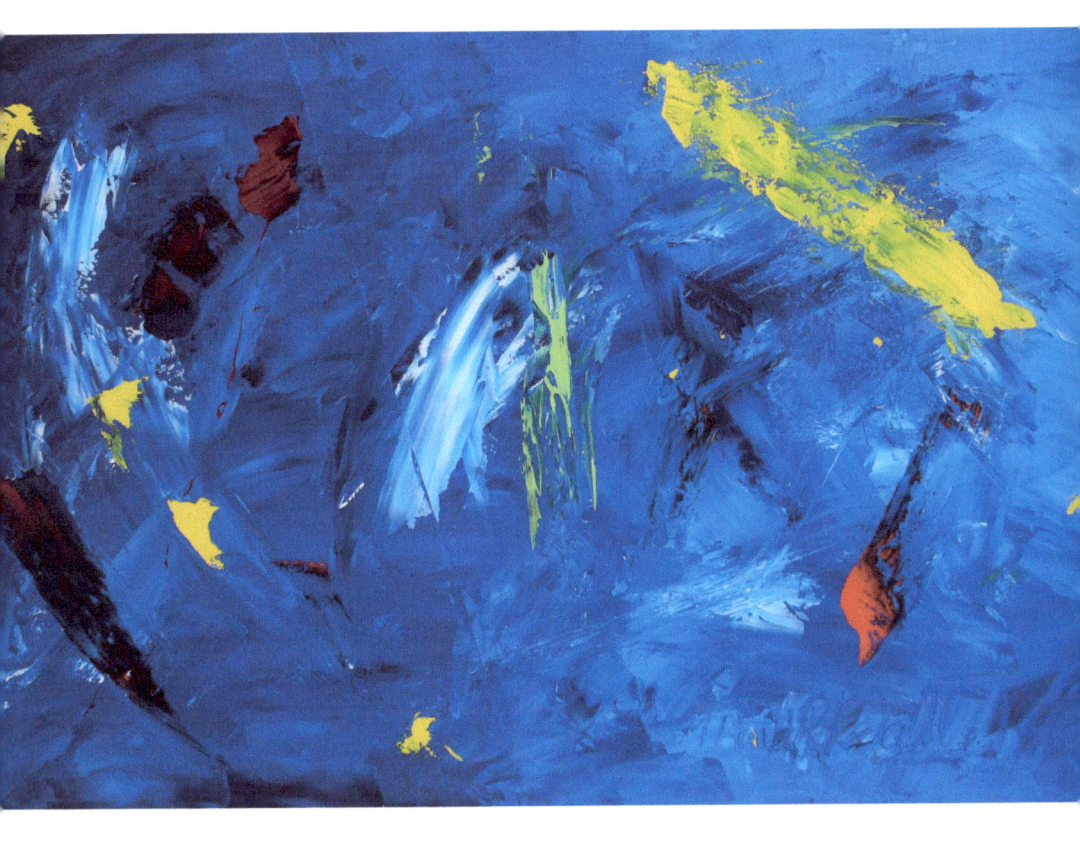

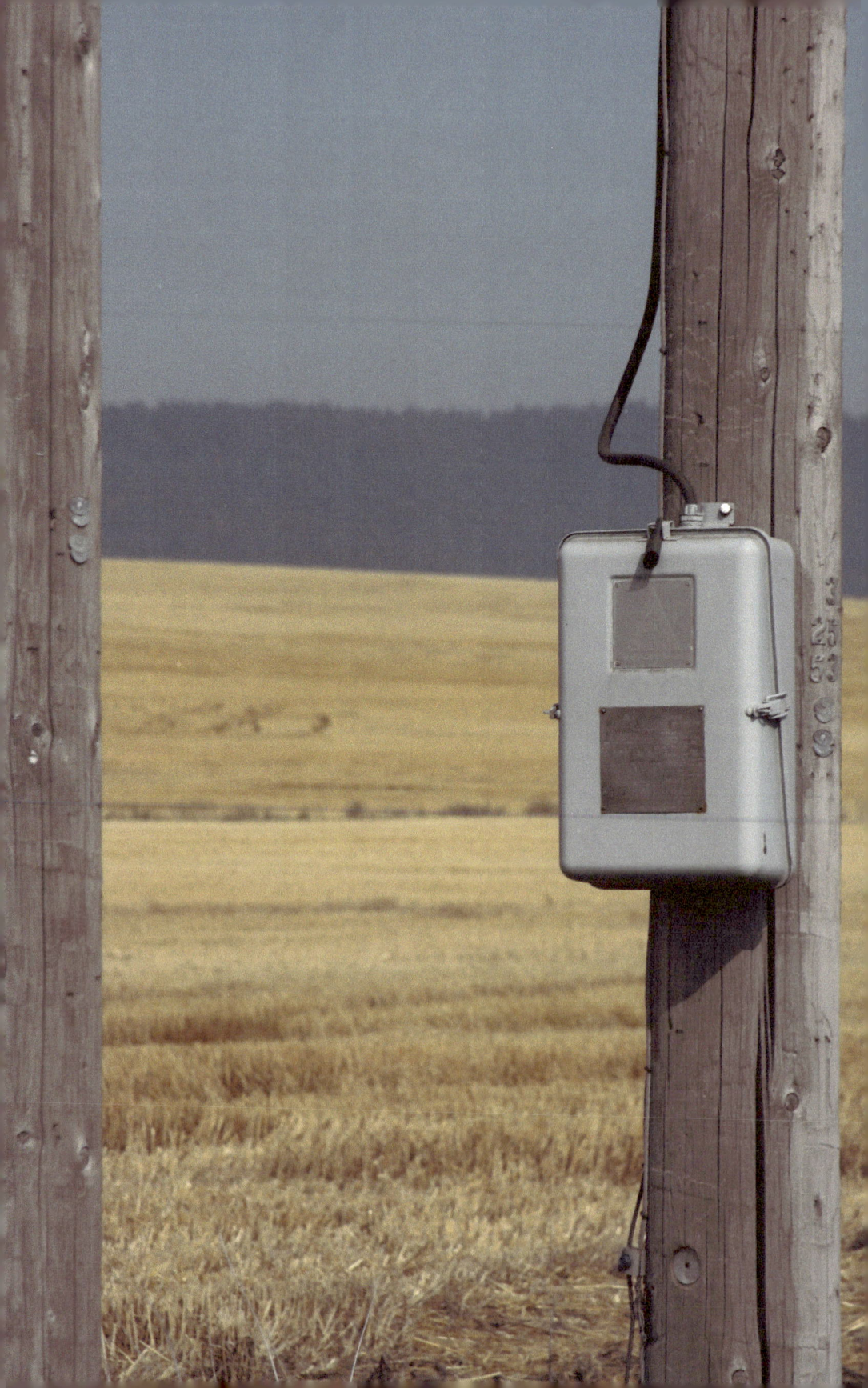

Gibbons usually like to swing from tree to tree. But the youngest gibbon in one family preferred adventures. He would swing in trees if it would get him to a new adventure. Otherwise he wasn't interested. As a result, all the gibbons he knew called him Monkey Brains. He called himself Little Gibbon, since he was still growing and learning lots.

One morning when he woke up, Little Gibbon wanted an adventure. But not one that was cold. And this morning Big Mountain was freezing.

Little Gibbon hiked down Big Mountain as fast as he could and headed straight for Big Desert. That looked like a place for a nice, warm adventure.

Little Gibbon had no water, no sunscreen, no compass and no sandals. He entered Big Desert smiling. Who needs those things when you want an adventure?

By now, you can probably guess what the answer is.

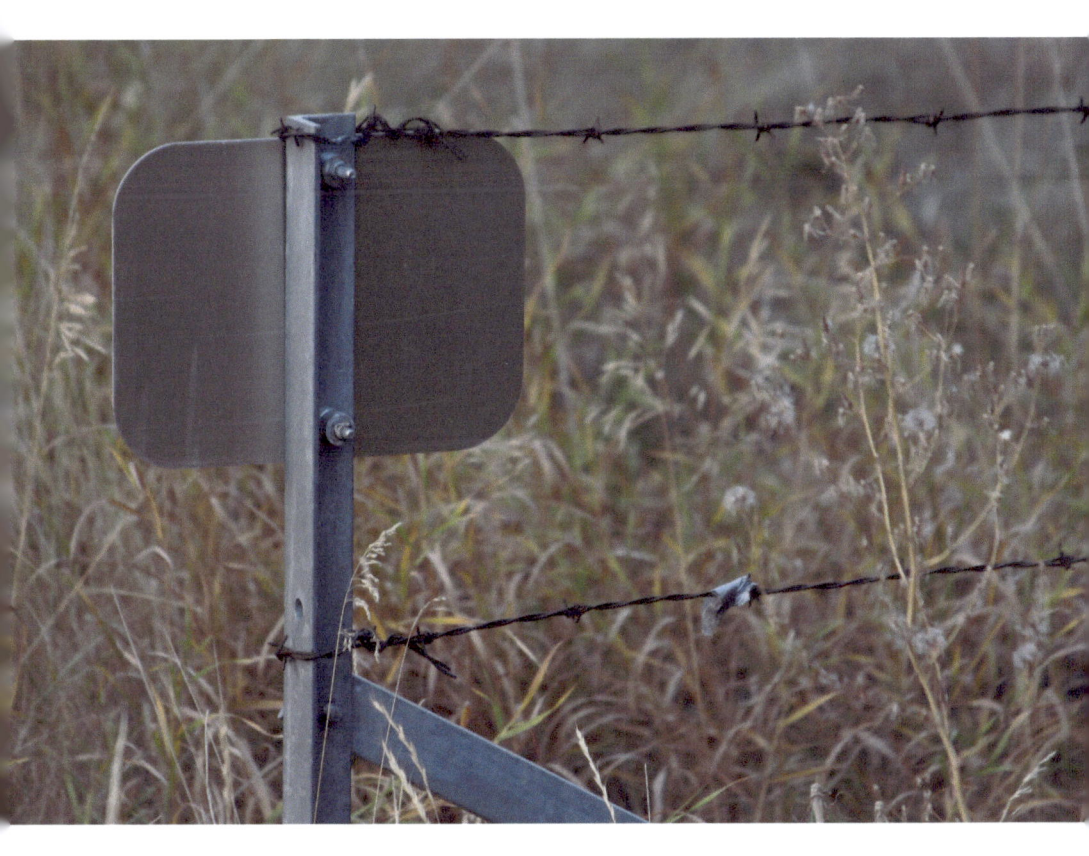

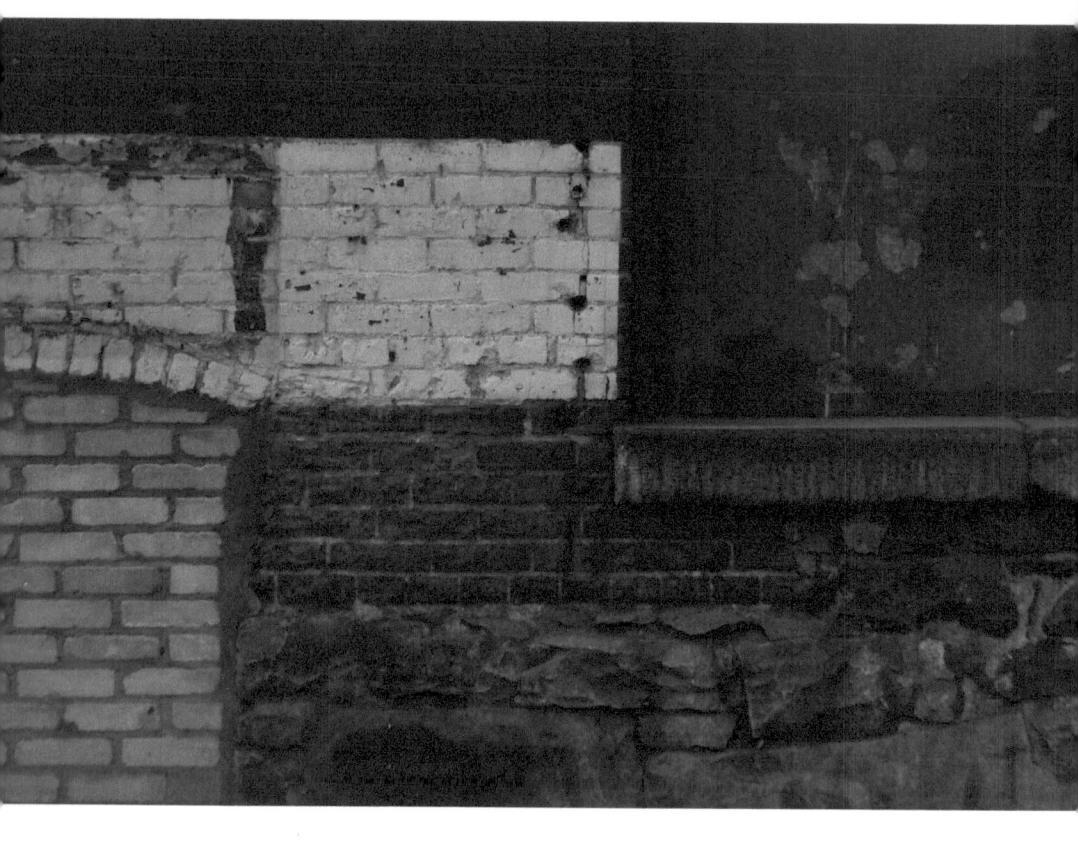

Luckily for Little Gibbon, Big Desert was in a good mood. Six months earlier Big Desert had been hot and oppressive, but those days were over. Now Big Desert was as temperate as he ever got. There was very little danger, as long as Little Gibbon stayed off Rattlesnake Hill.

By now you probably know where Little Gibbon went.

Little Gibbon saw a bit of rock, not big enough to be a mountain, more of a hill than anything else. Little Gibbon smiled. He headed straight for it. He was going to have an adventure!

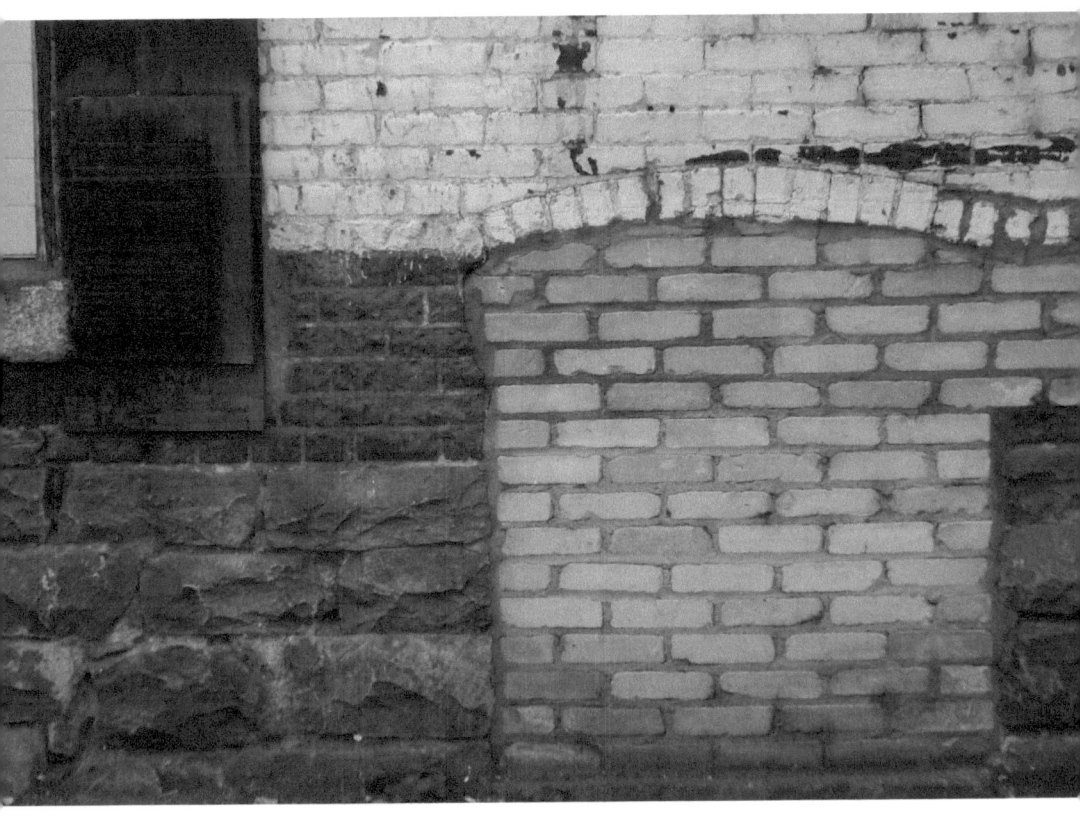

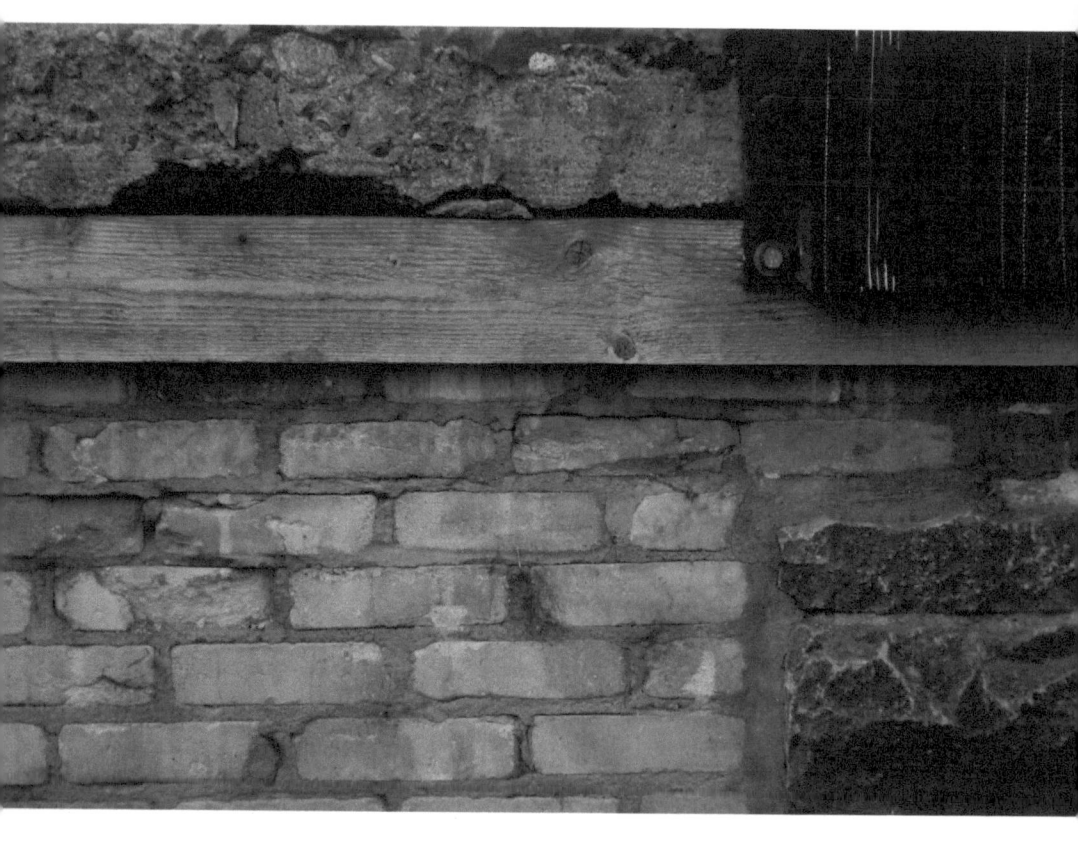

As Little Gibbon started climbing Rattlesnake Hill, the air was calm and still. It was very quiet all around him. Then Little Gibbon heard a whirring noise, like a rattle, quite close. Then he heard another. And another. It was like a beautiful percussion concert. Little Gibbon was delighted at the sound.

"Big Desert!" Little Gibbon shouted. "We're having an adventure!"

Big Desert smiled and held his breath. He never knew what would happen when Little Gibbon was around.

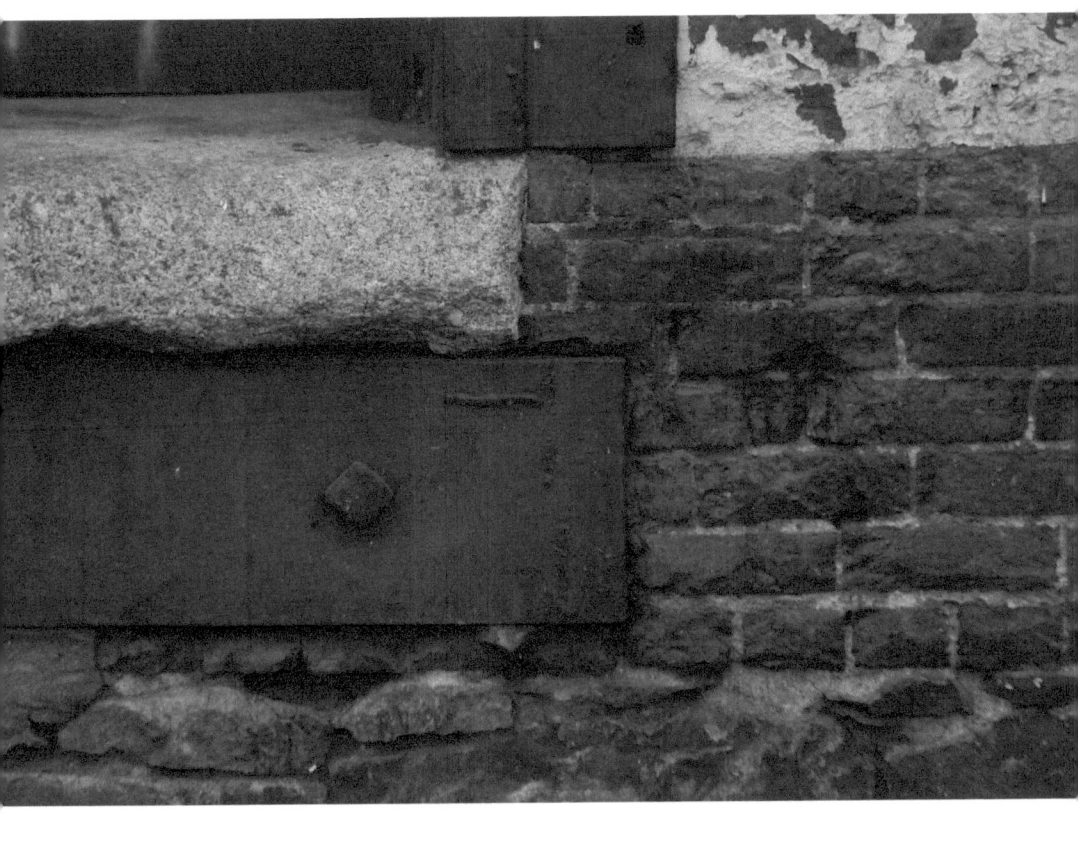

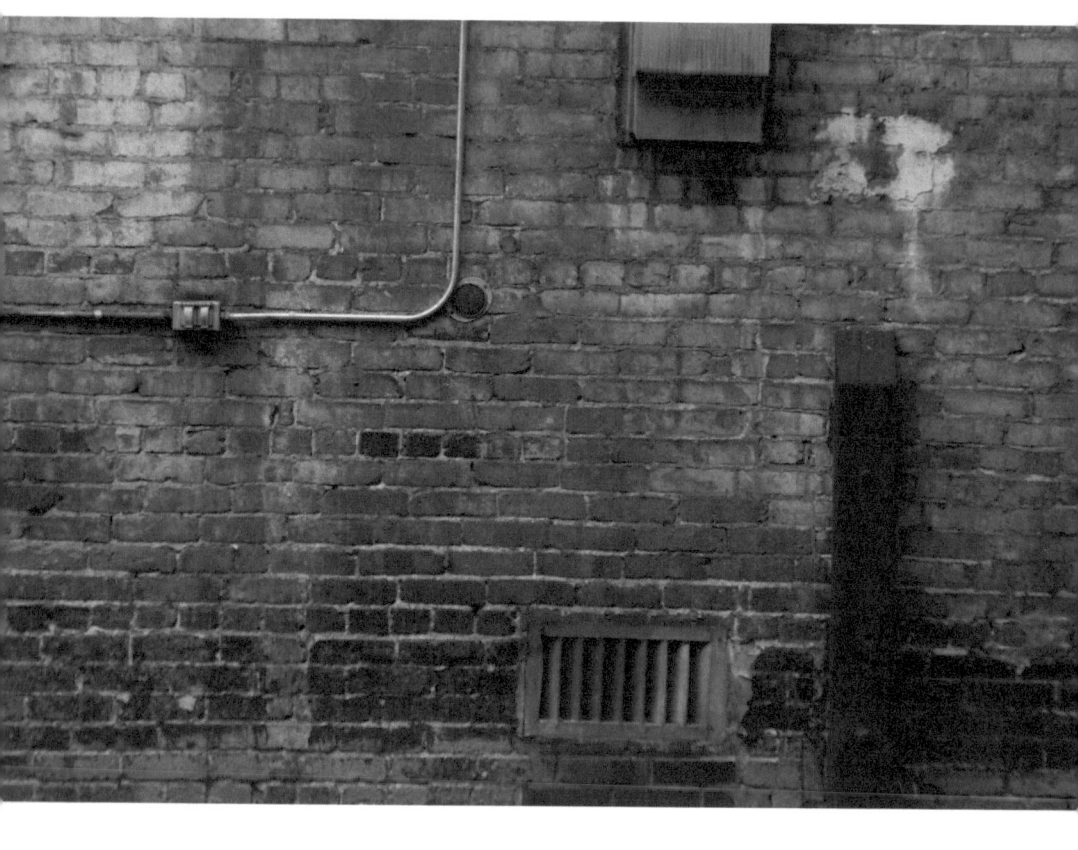

Little Gibbon glanced down. He saw a rattlesnake ahead of him shaking his tail. He looked left. *Another* rattlesnake, shaking his tail. He looked right. *Another* rattlesnake, shaking his tail. They all looked mean and very unhappy.

Little Gibbon glanced behind him. No snakes there. He backed up, carefully watching for unhappy snakes.

As he retreated, the snakes quit shaking their tails, and the air became quiet again.

"Big Desert!" Little Gibbon shouted. "We're having an adventure!"

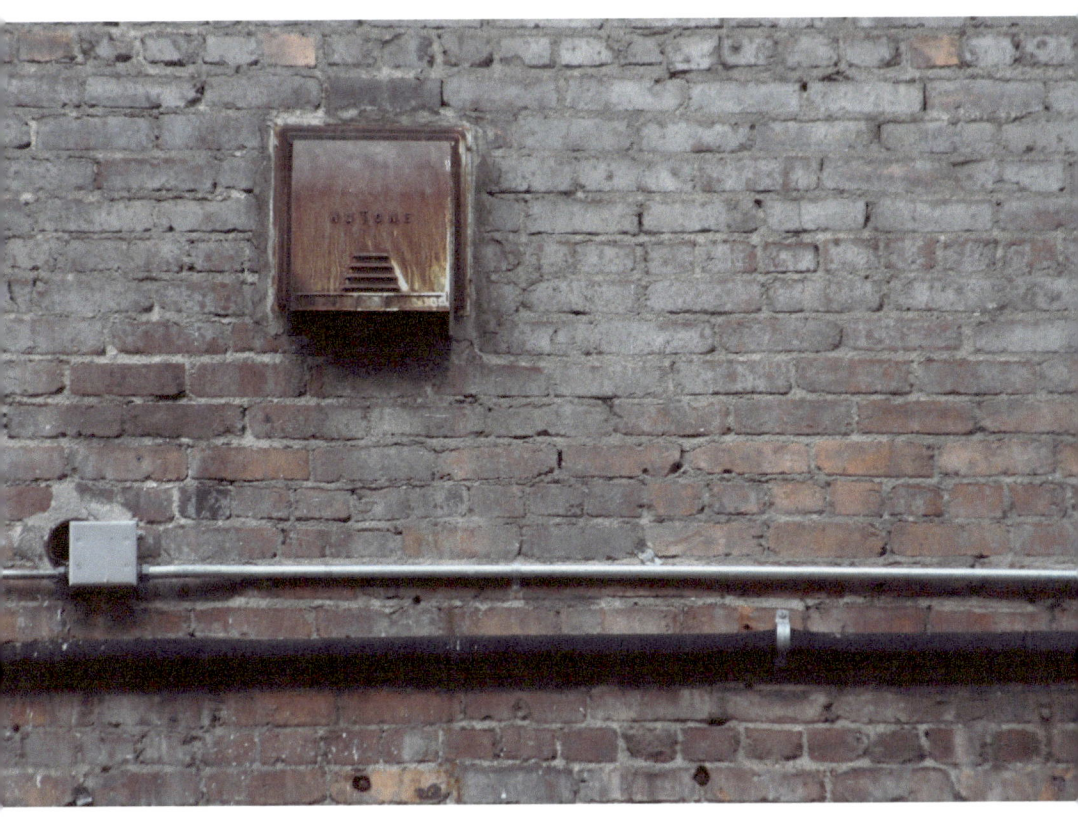

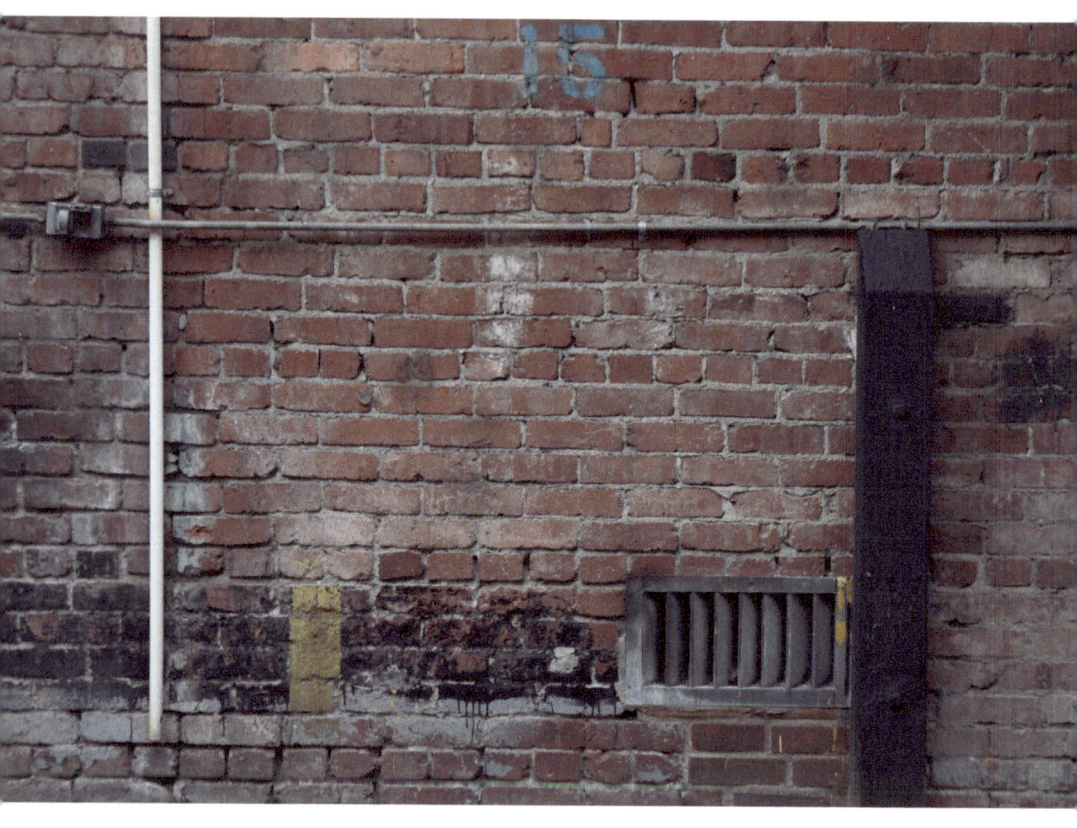

Big Desert sighed. He thought things would be better, now that Little Gibbon had moved away from Rattlesnake Hill. The rest of the desert was mostly free of rattlesnakes and posed no real danger, except for the Prickly Cactus Maze.

Little Gibbon looked ahead to see what was coming up. He saw some nice cacti about four feet high.

Little Gibbon admired a large prickly pear cactus when he passed it. Close beside was a lovely golden barrel cactus. Then a large pencil cholla. By the time Little Gibbon came to the fishhook barrel cactus, he had to squeeze sideways so he didn't get stuck. Soon he found it difficult to walk *anywhere* without bumping into cactus needles.

"Ouch!" Little Gibbon exclaimed. He had been doing his best to avoid bumping into cacti, but a cholla had just jumped onto his leg. At least that's what it seemed like. "Ouch! Ouch! Ouch!"

Little Gibbon was in the maze for a long time before he found his way out. When he finally got to a rock outside the maze, he sat down and pulled cactus spines out of his legs, arms and feet. He wasn't distressed. He was happy. You probably know why.

"Big Desert!" he shouted. "We're having an adventure!"

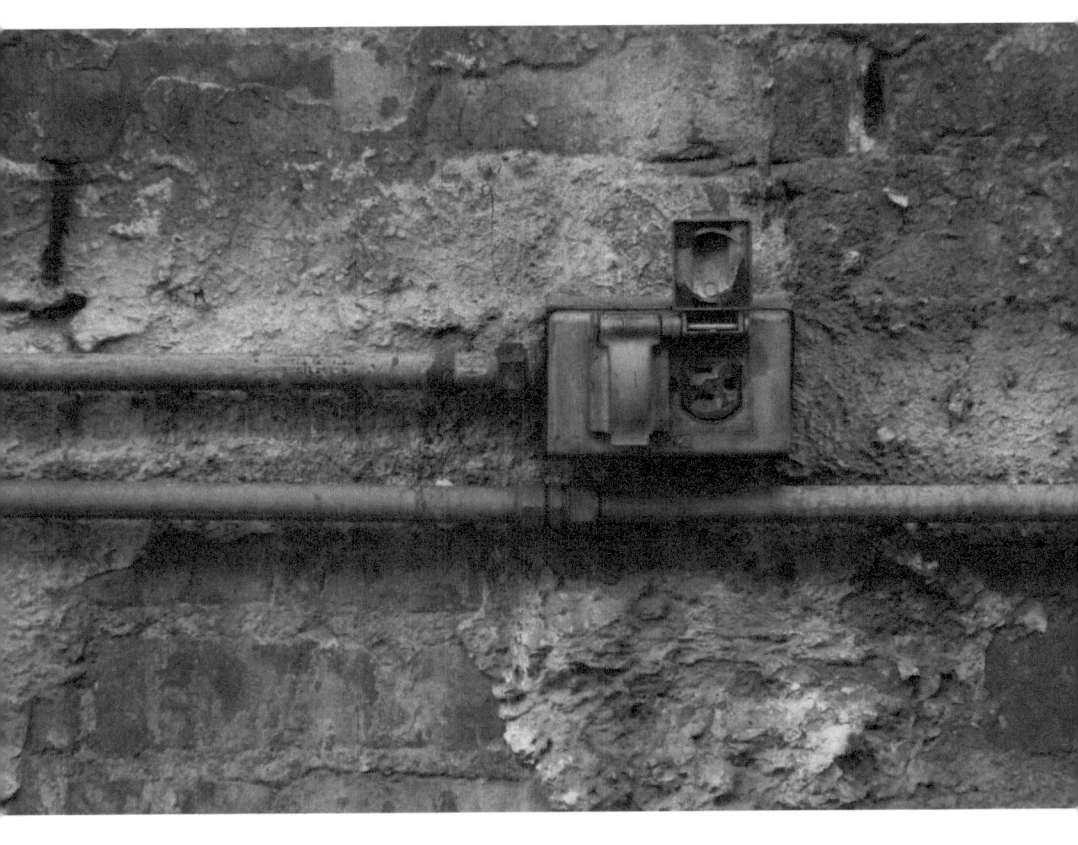

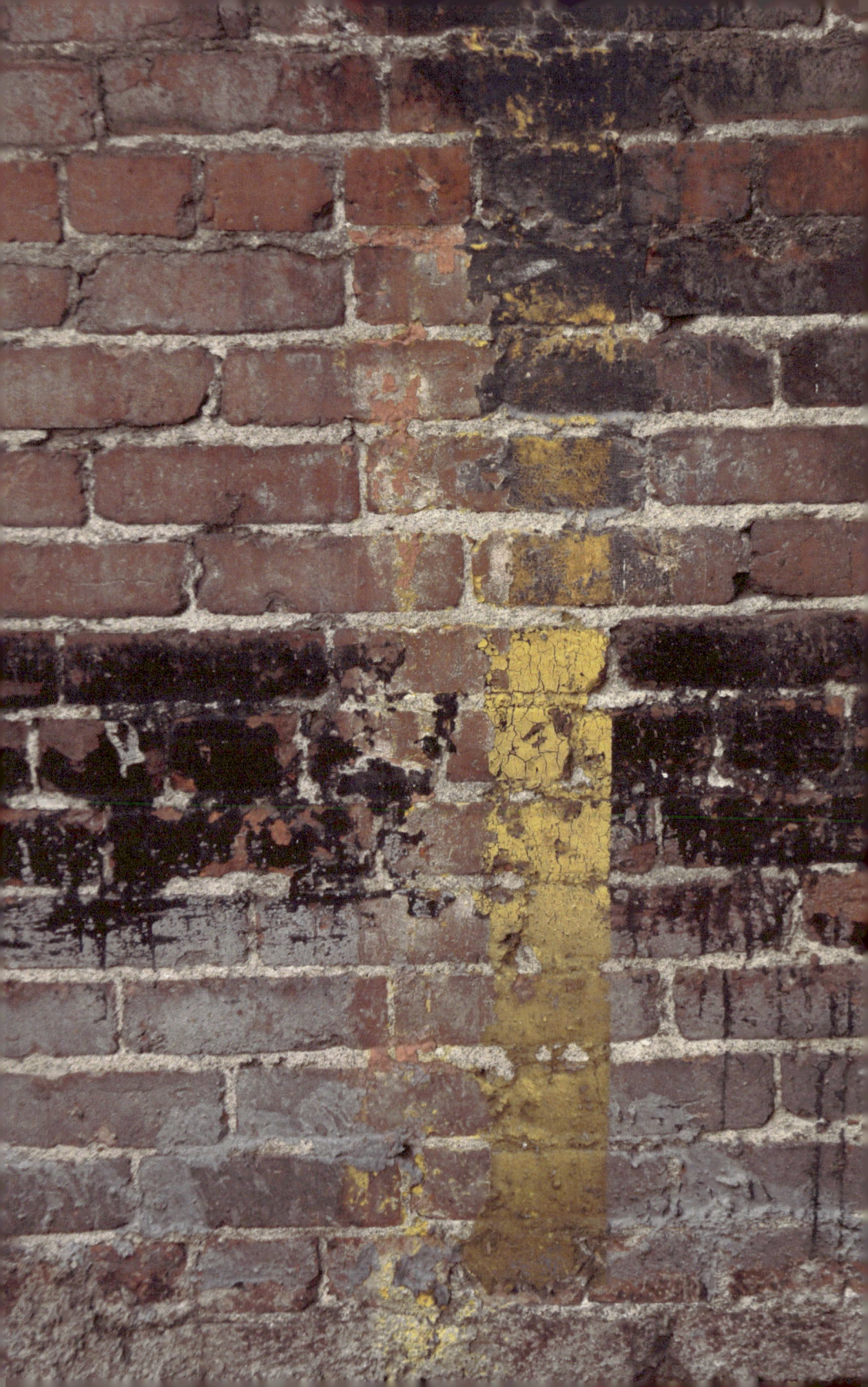

Big Desert sighed. He thought things would be better, now that Little Gibbon was past Rattlesnake Hill and Prickly Cactus Maze. As long as Little Gibbon kept drinking water and wore sunscreen and had a hat, there was not really that much danger from the Hot Blazing Sun.

Big Desert looked and saw that Little Gibbon didn't have a canteen for water. He didn't have any sunscreen. He didn't have a hat.

"Big Desert!" Little Gibbon shouted. "I'm getting thirsty! I'm glad I see water ahead!"

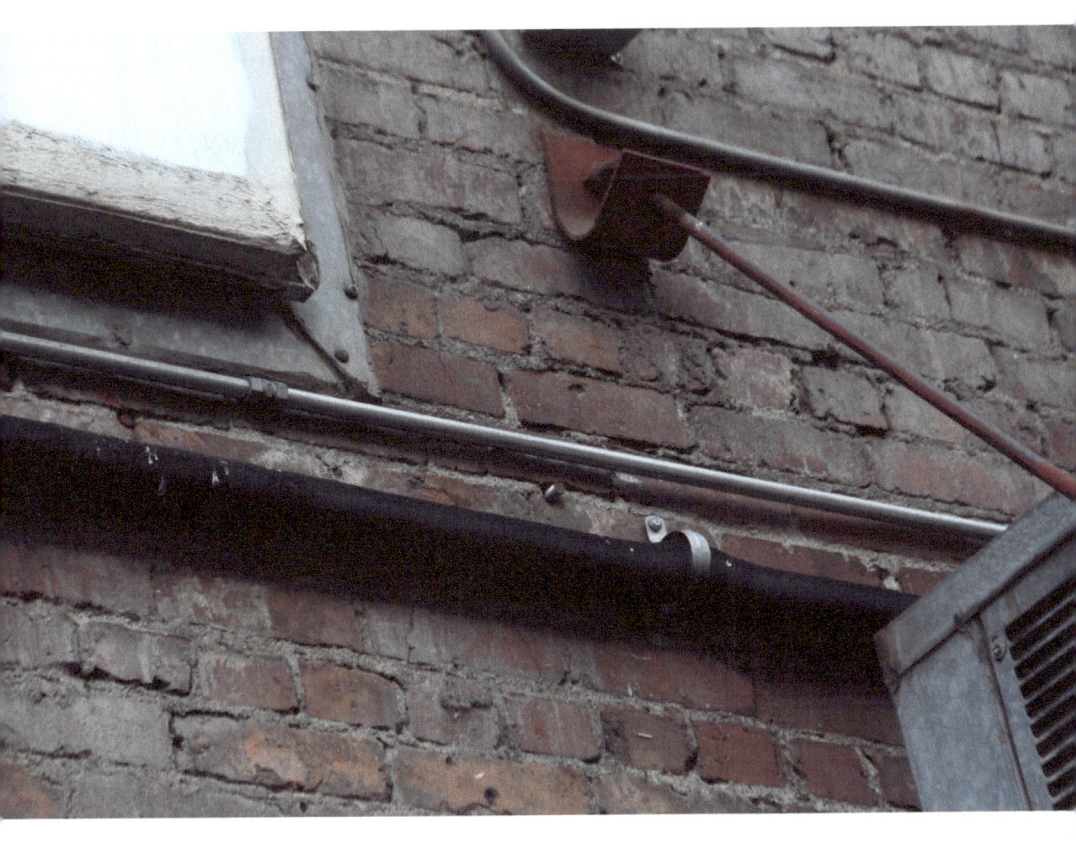

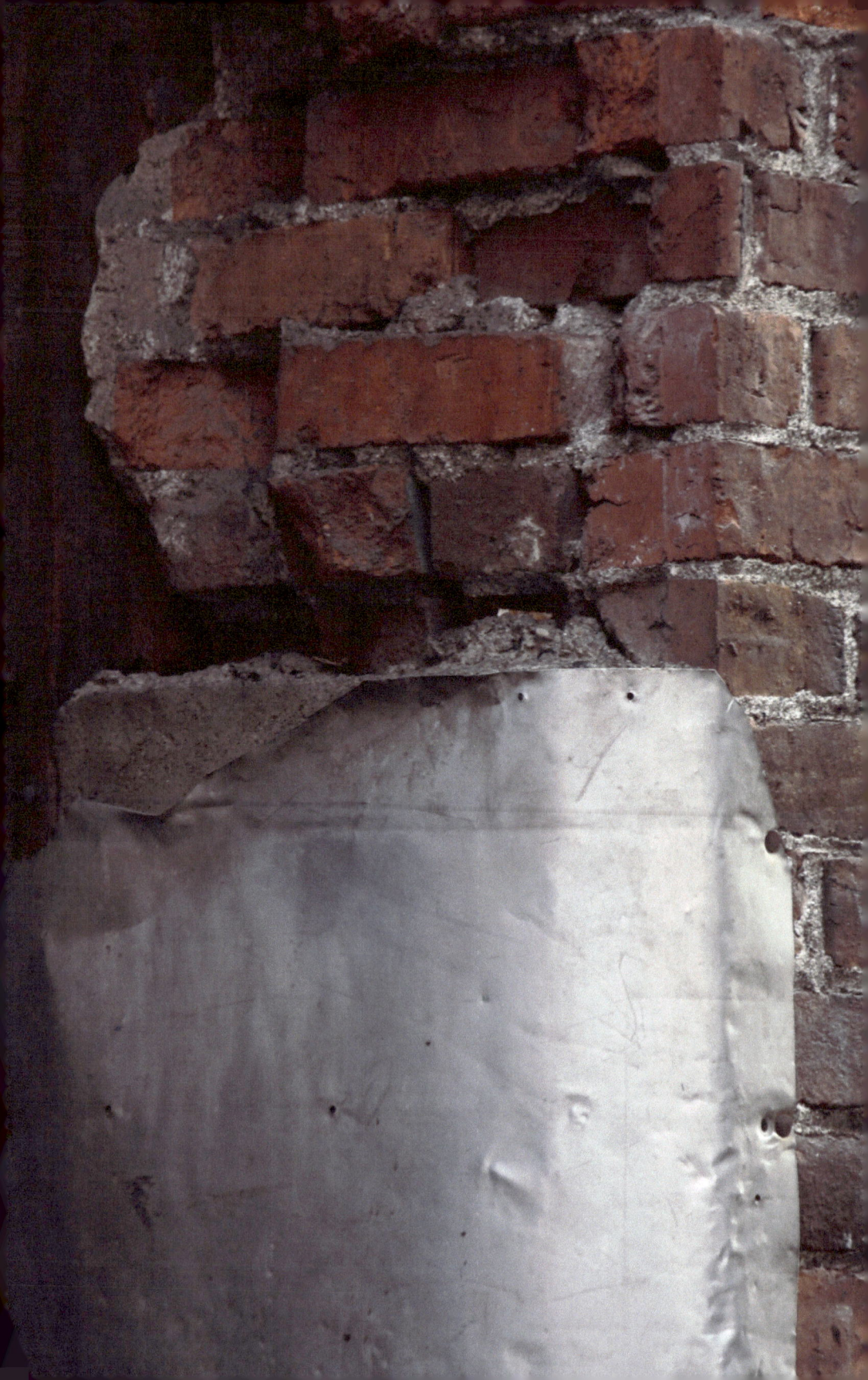

Big Desert looked. *He* didn't see water ahead. It was just a game Big Sun liked to play. Big Sun drew pictures of water on Big Desert.

Little Gibbon went from one shimmering image of water to the next, getting more thirsty as he went. His trip in Big Desert was not quite as much fun as he thought it would be.

"Big Desert!" Little Gibbon sputtered. "This is almost *too much* of an adventure!"

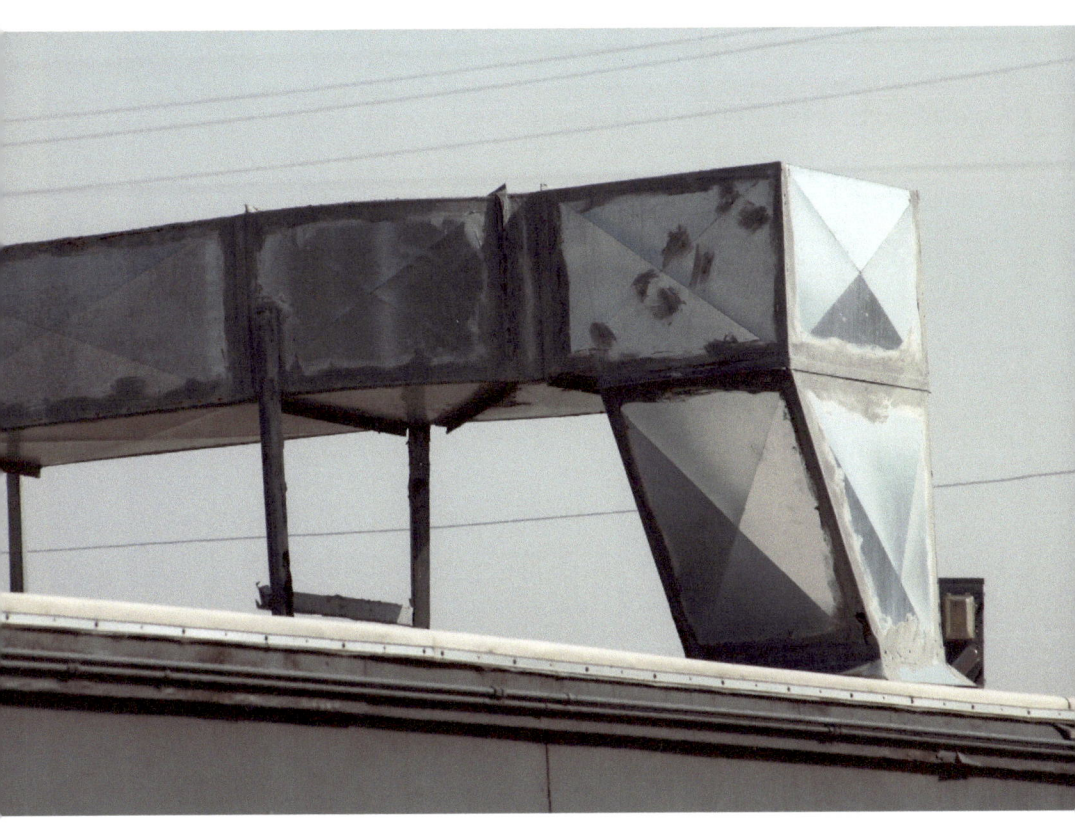

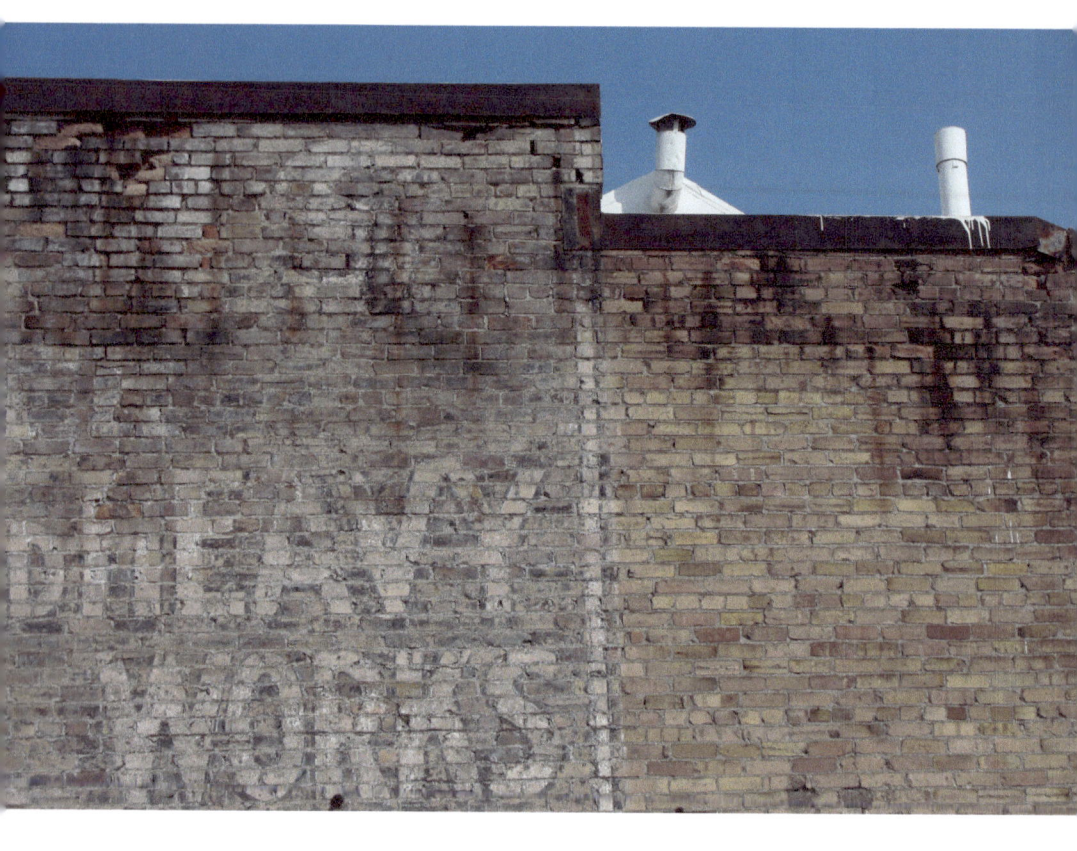

Big Desert was relieved when four o'clock came. After four, the heat started to decrease. There was almost no danger now that Little Gibbon was safely past Rattlesnake Hill and the Prickly Cactus Maze and soon would be out of the Hot Blazing Sun. About the only thing that could go wrong was if Little Gibbon lay down in the Cave Filled With Stinging Scorpions.

"Big Desert!" Little Gibbon shouted. "That's enough adventure for today. I'm going to take a nap out of the sun in that nice cave I see up ahead."

All the scorpions scuttled out of view as Little Gibbon approached.

Little Gibbon entered the cave, smiled, and lay down for a nap.

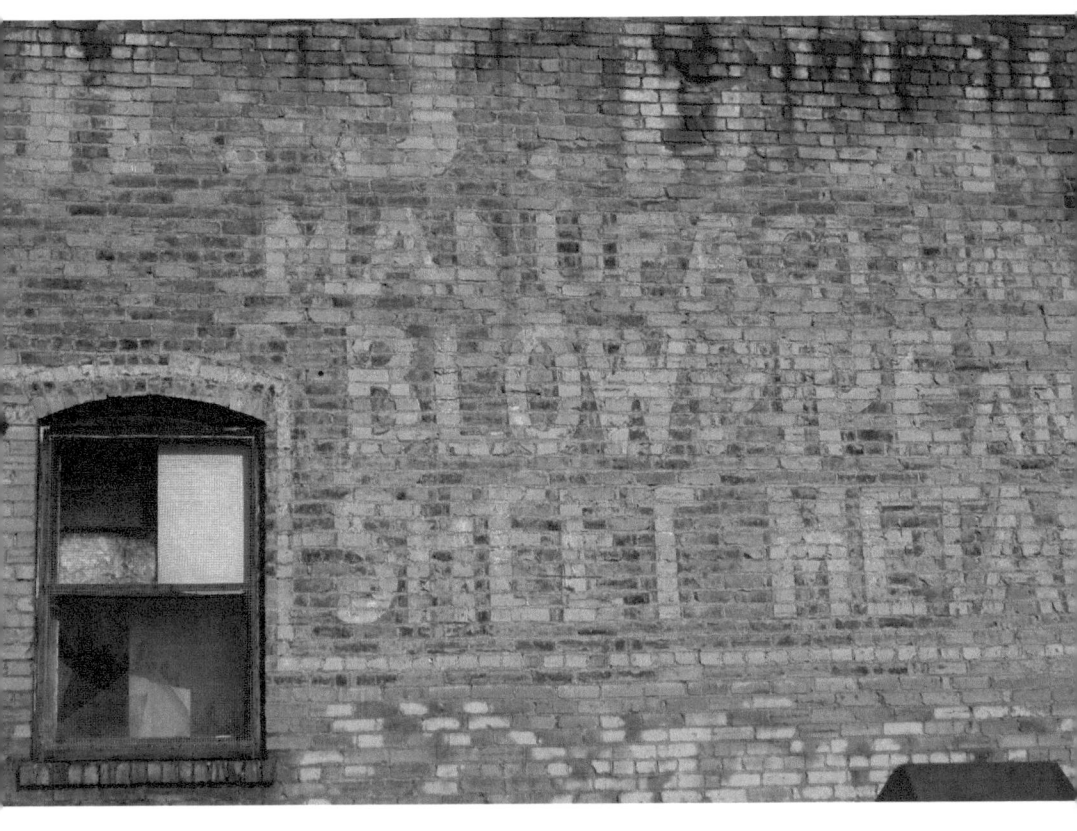

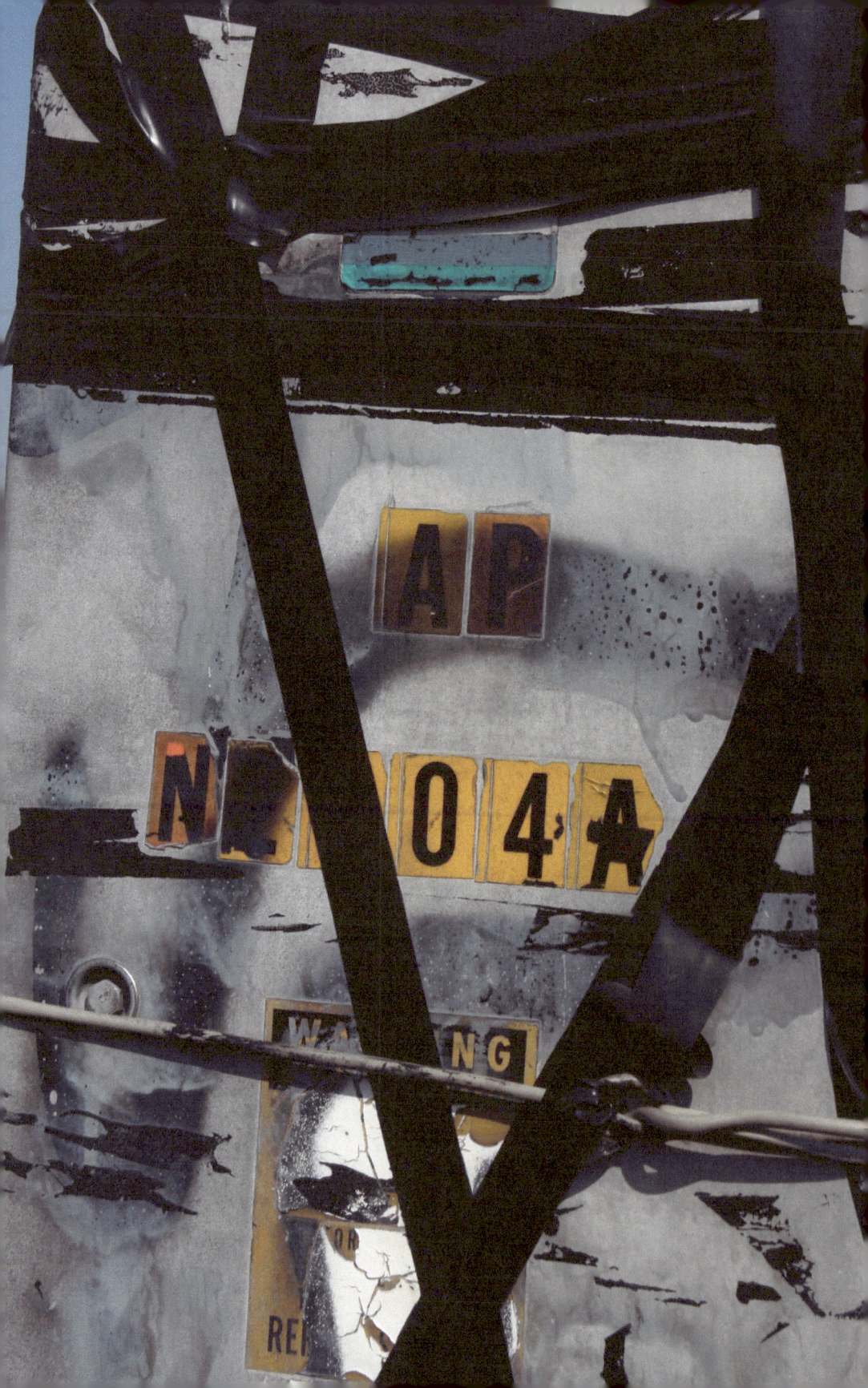

Little Gibbon was just starting to fall asleep when he remembered that he had gone to Big Desert to have an adventure, not to take naps. He could sleep anytime.

Little Gibbon hopped up. He saw a palm tree a little ways away. He headed for that, and was surprised (and delighted) to find a small pool of water near the base of the palm when he arrived.

Little Gibbon took a slurp of water, then watched as the little pool slowly filled back up. He got another drink and watched the pool fill up again. After a few minutes, Little Gibbon had gotten quite a big drink, a little bit at a time. Then he climbed the palm tree to see what he could.

Little Gibbon found the leaves at the top *very* comfortable and he was so contented after his drink and so warm that he fell asleep. He didn't mean to, but he did. It was time for his nap.

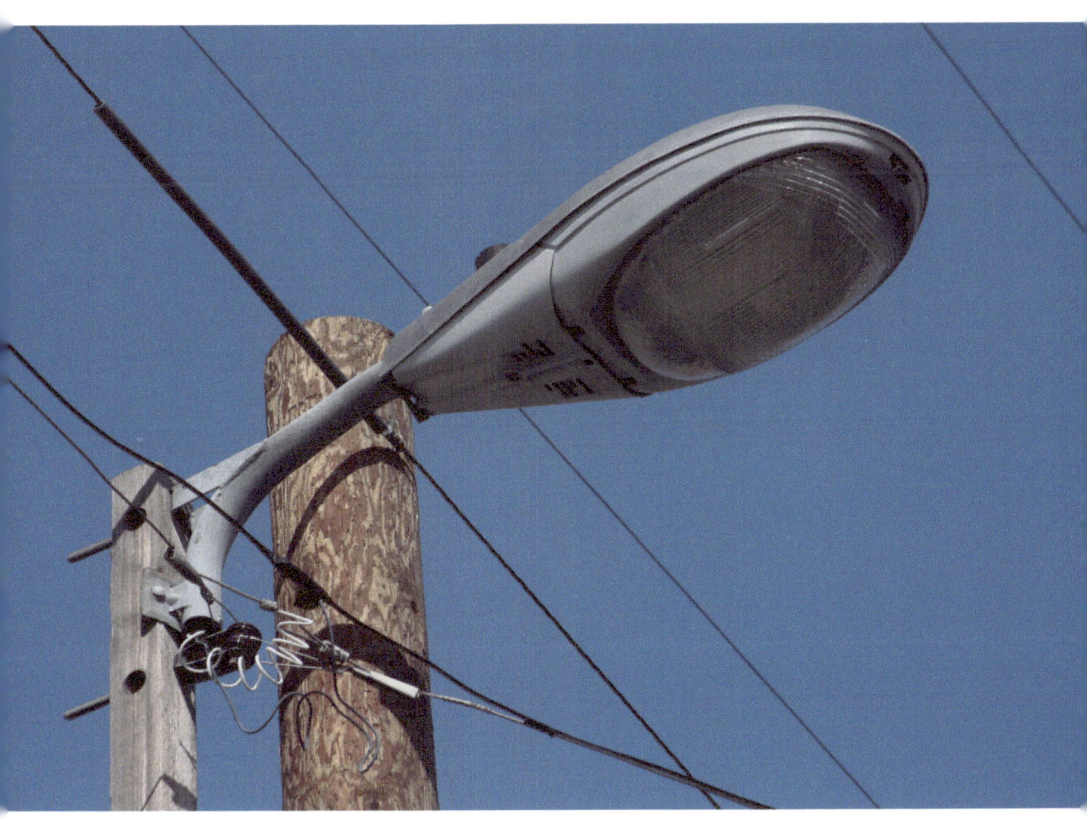

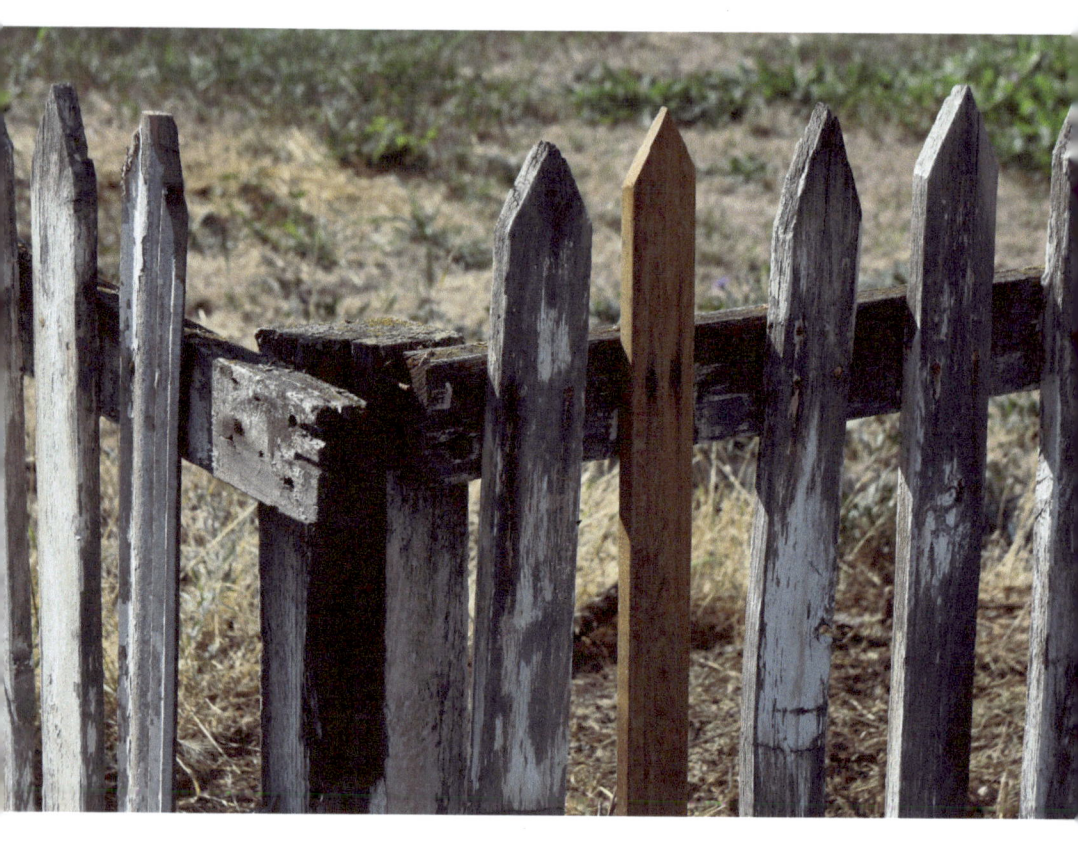

Big Desert smiled and watched Little Gibbon sleep on the top of the palm tree. Big Desert didn't wake Little Gibbon while he rearranged the Shifting Sand Dunes, making it impossible to see any tracks back to Big Mountain.

Big Desert didn't wake Little Gibbon when the Howling Coyote Pack wandered past, disappointed that Little Gibbon was safely at the top of the tree.

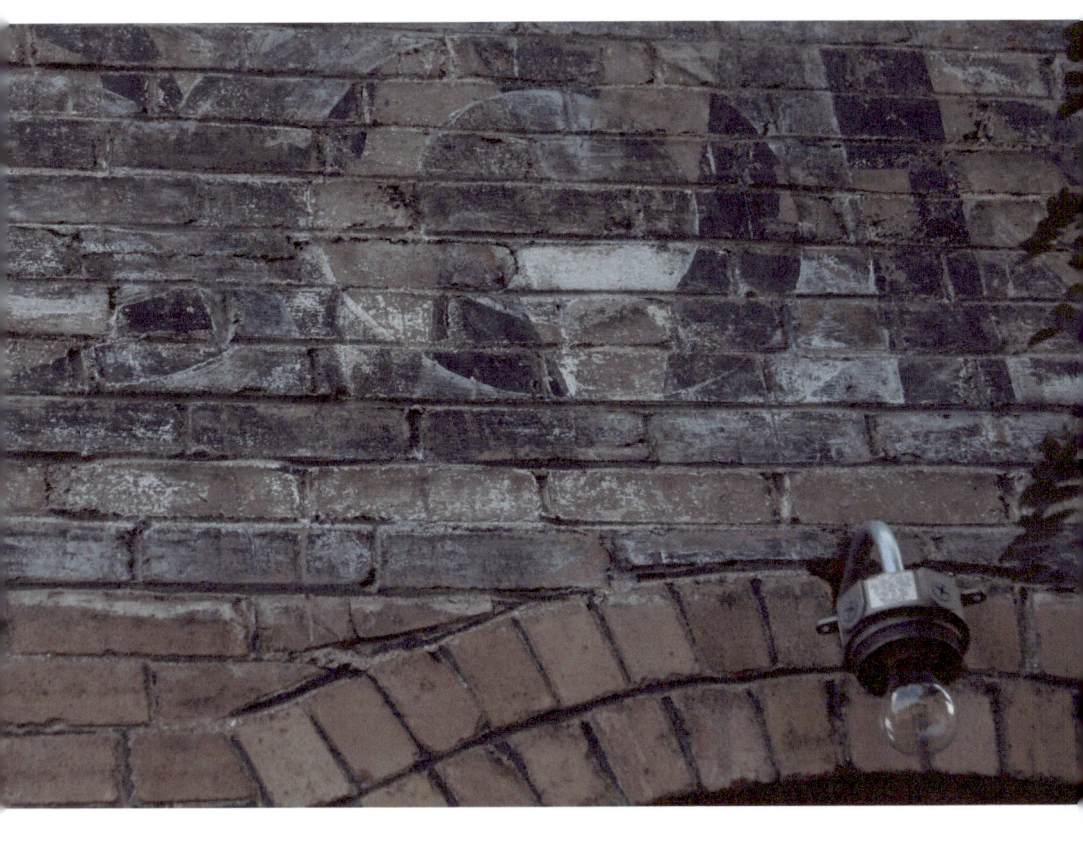

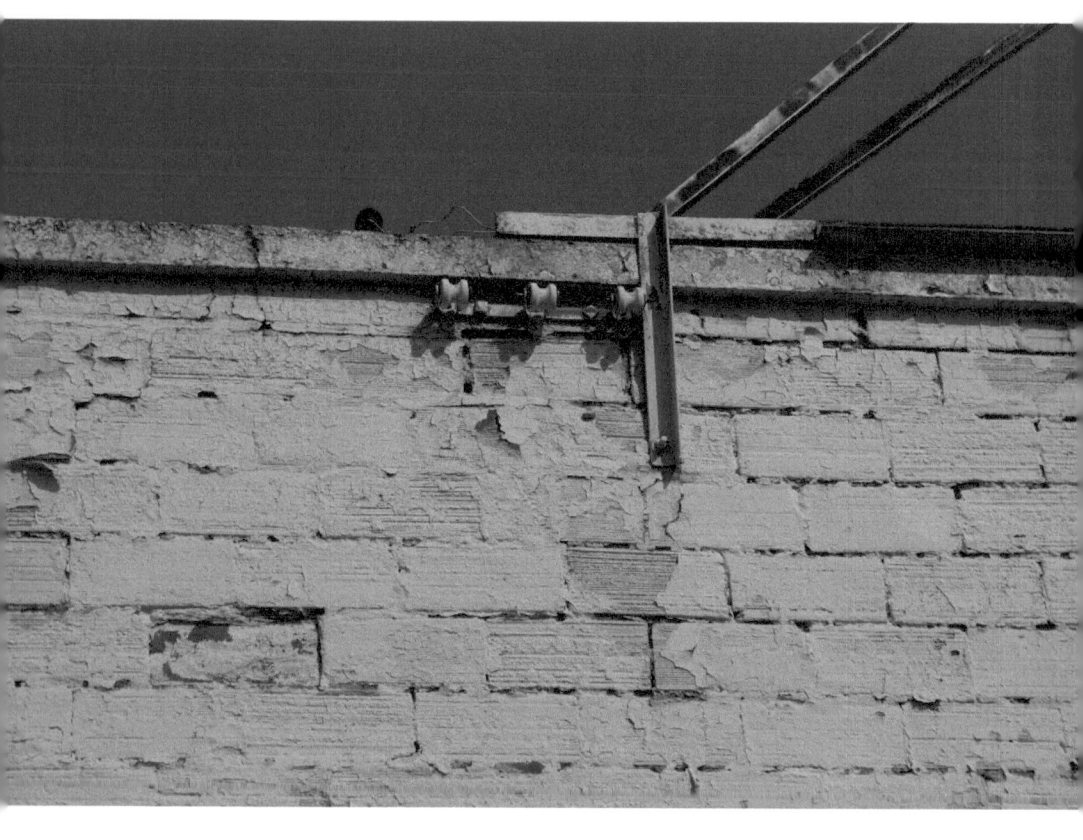

Big Desert didn't wake Little Gibbon when the Freezing Night Temperatures arrived. Little Gibbon was warm enough, comfortably covered by palm leaves.

Little Gibbon had had enough adventures for one day, thought Big Desert. There was always tomorrow.

~~

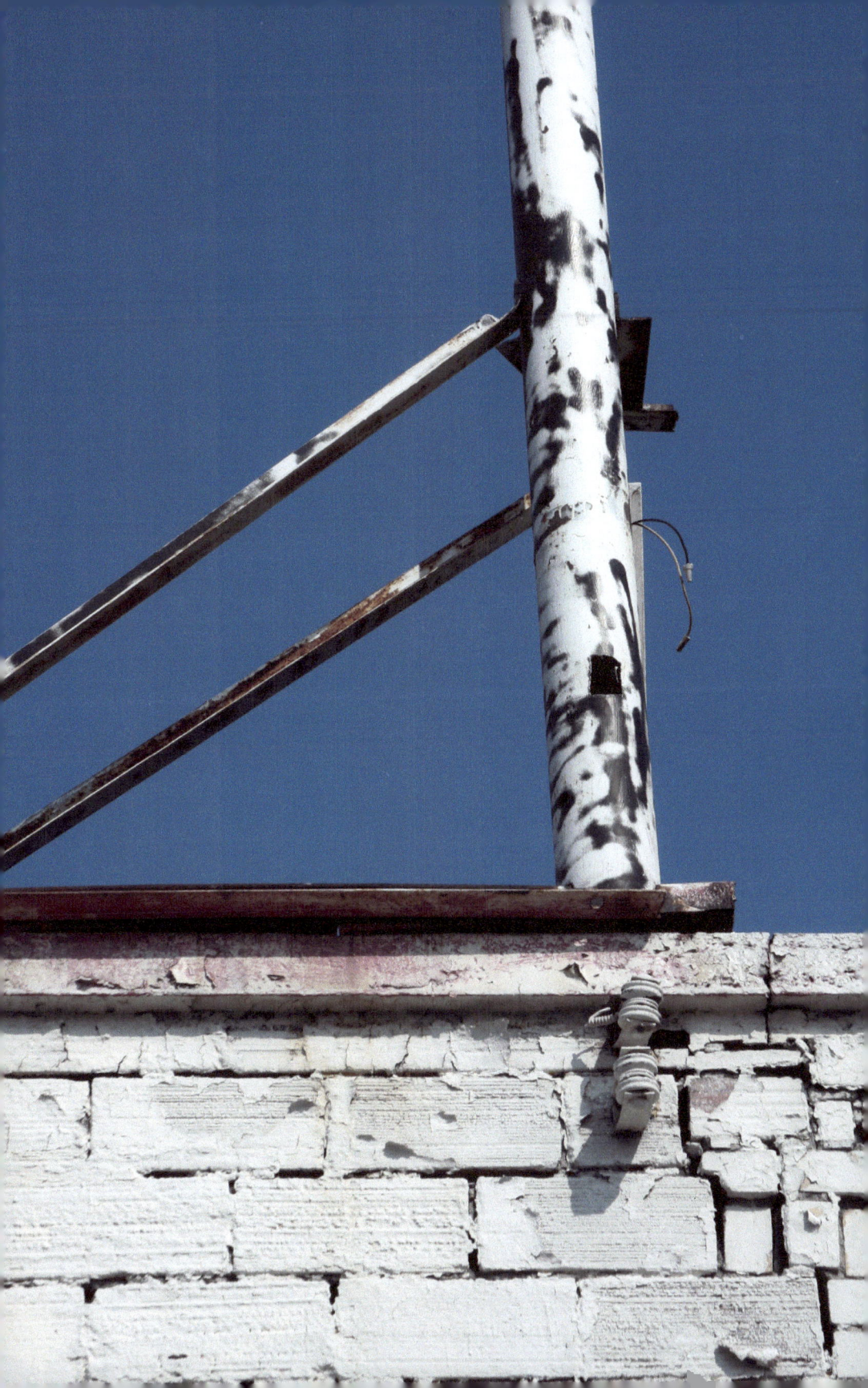

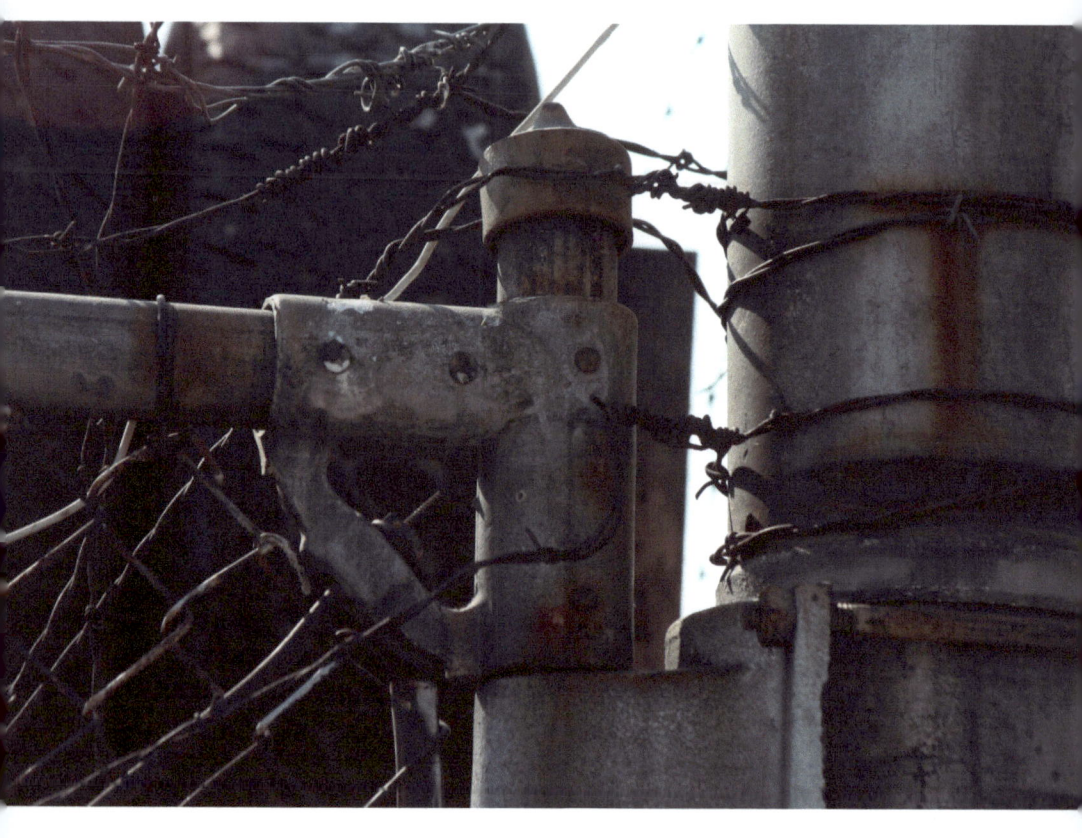

Reflection questions

When have you been uncomfortable on an adventure?

When have you been surprised on an adventure?

When have you been delighted?

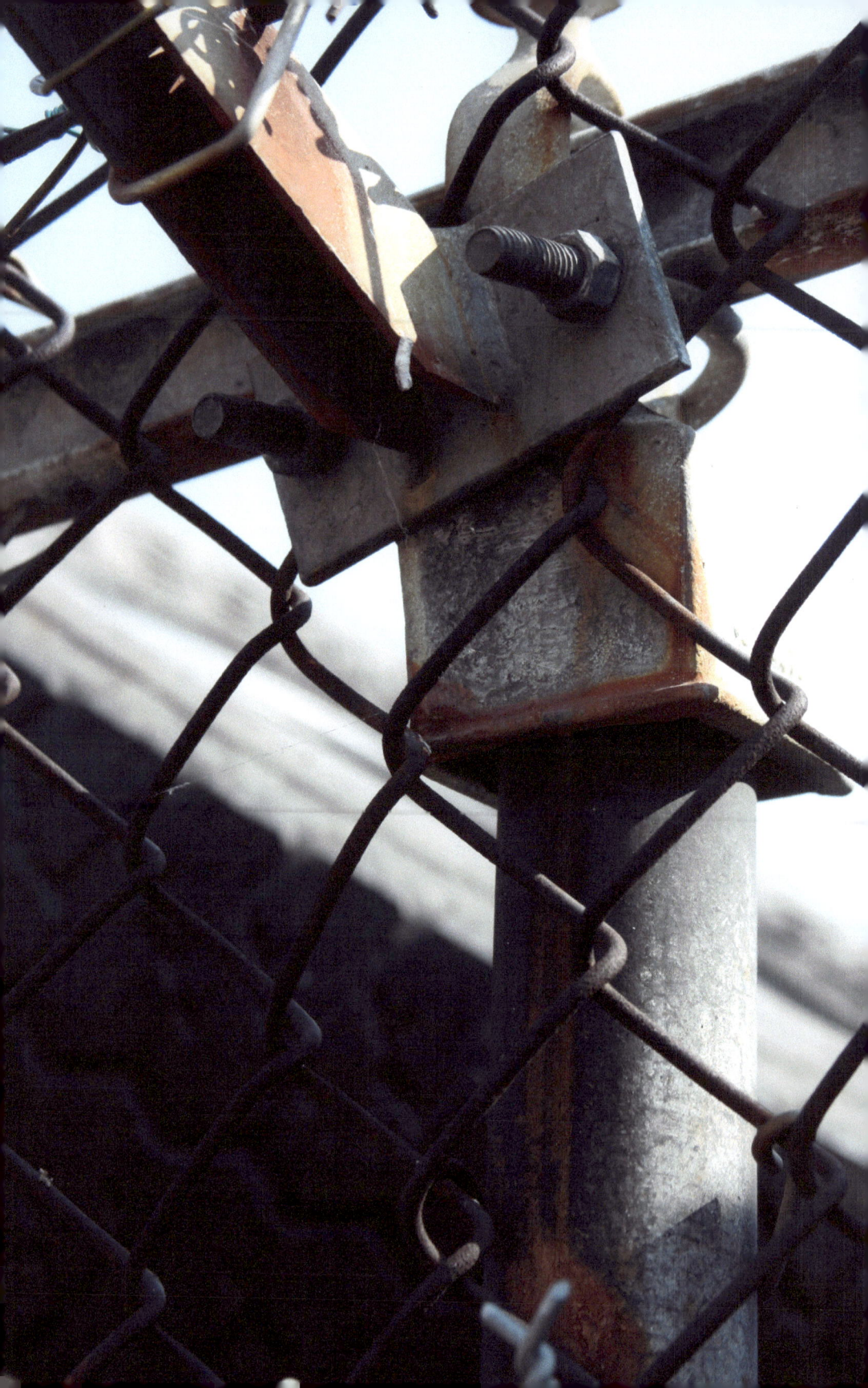

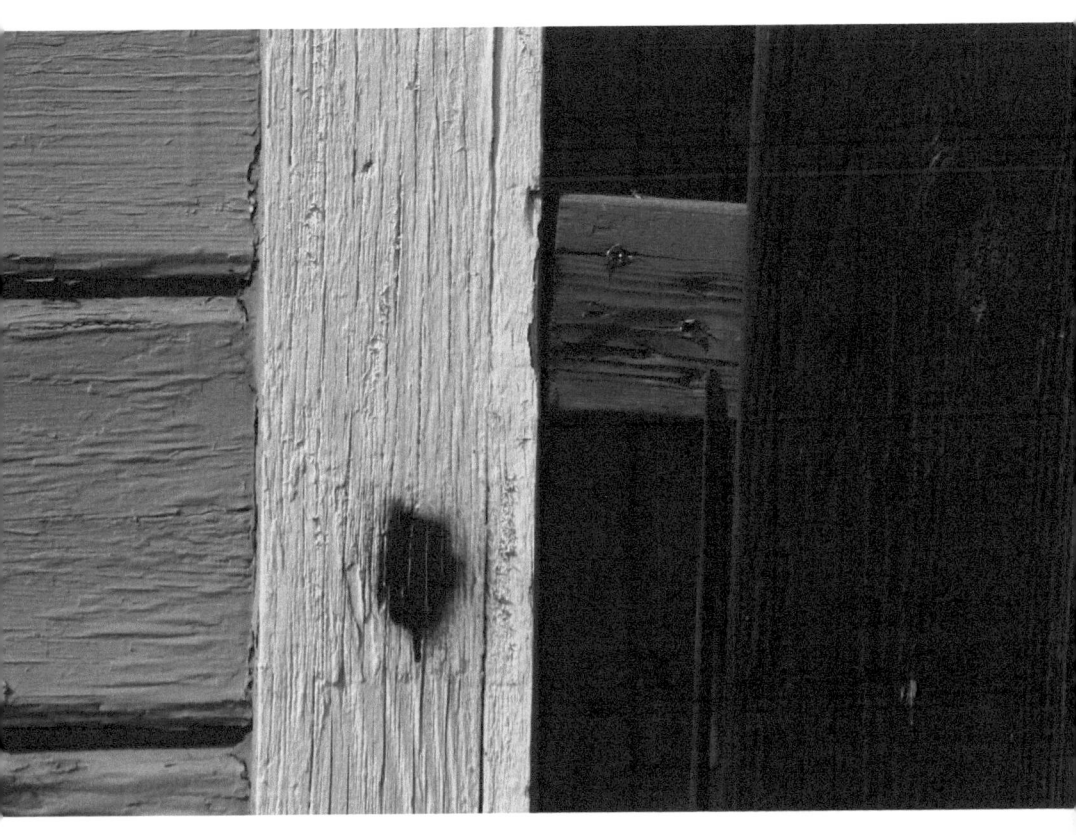

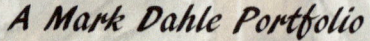

A Mark Dahle Portfolio

Amanda Gets A Pumpkin

(#1 in the series "Amanda Wanted A Miracle")

This Mark Dahle Portfolio includes a colorful painting, twenty-four beautiful industrial photographs from Beijing, Shangahi and Xian, and a story about a girl who wanted a miracle.

"Oh dear," said her grandmother. "You didn't want a pumpkin? Perhaps we'll have to try again."

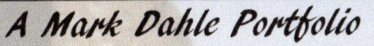

A Mark Dahle Portfolio

Farmer Jane

This Mark Dahle Portfolio includes a beautiful painting, twenty-five gorgeous photographs from the Netherlands, and a story about Farmer Jane.

Jane didn't know that farmers have troubles.

But she was about to discover how *many* troubles they have.

This Mark Dahle Portfolio includes a gorgeous abstract painting, twenty-five beautiful photographs of construction in Basel, Switzerland, and a story about a group of trolls moving to Norway.

When the trolls moved, they had to pass through a large forest. The trees and the trolls kept bumping into each other. It was no fault of the trees.

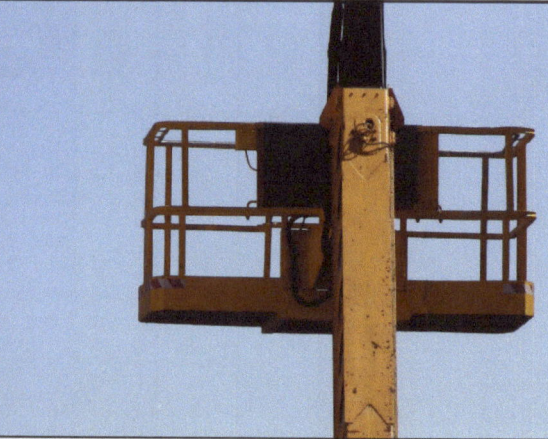

A Mark Dahle Portfolio

When The Trolls Moved

www.ingramcontent.com/pod-product-compliance
Lightning Source LLC
Chambersburg PA
CBHW040901180526
45159CB00001B/481